TEMPORARY HELP

TEMPORARY HELP

POEMS BY JOHN ENGMAN

HOLY COW! PRESS · DULUTH, MINNESOTA · 1998

We gratefully acknowledge the support of many generous individuals for this project:
Elmer L. Andersen, Carolyn M. Bacon, John S. Batalden, George Cossette, Jennifer
Crosby, Cass Dalglish & Natasha D'Schommer, Jim Dochniak, Peter J. Eckberg, William V.
Frame, Douglas E. Green, Mara Kirk Hart, Kathleen A. Holliday, Robert Karlen, Chuck
& Nancy Maland, Ethna M. McKiernan, Marie O. Mc Neff, John R. Mitchell, Richard C.
Nelson, Ron Palosaari, Anne Panning, John-Mark & Nancy Stensvaag, Saul & Mary
Stensvaag, Clair & Gladys Strommen, Ralph L. Sulerud, Barton Sutter, Robert H. Tesarek,
Deacon & Jenny Warner, Thomas Zarth.

Library of Congress Cataloging-in-Publication Data

Engman, John, 1949-1996
    Temporary help : poems / John Engman.
       p.   cm.
    ISBN 0-930100-82-4
    I. Title.
PS3555.M475T46   1998
811'.54—dc21   98-2600
                                  CIP

Holy Cow! Press books are distributed to the trade by Consortium Book Sales and Distri-
bution, 1045 Westgate Drive, Saint Paul, Minnesota, 55114. Our books are also available
through all major library distributors and jobbers, and through most small press distribu-
tors including Bookpeople and Small Press Distribution. For personal orders, catalogs or
other information, write to: Holy Cow! Press, Post Office Box 3170, Mount Royal Station,
Duluth, Minnesota 55803.

ACKNOWLEDGMENTS

Grateful acknowledgment to the editors of the following publications in which these poems first appeared:

Agassiz Review: "Sobbing Uncontrollably in Public Places"
Caliban: "Terrible Weather Conditions"
Chiaroscuro: "Money," "After Watching Korean Children Dying on Black & White Television, 1953"
Crazyhorse: "The Longest Sidewalk in the Western World," "What I Remember of What They Told Me"
the eleventh MUSE: "Aluminum Folding Chairs"
The Green Mountain Review: "The Window in the Cow"
Indiana Review: "Goldfish at Loring Pond"
Minnesota Writes: Poetry: "Another Word for Blue"
New England Review/Bread Loaf Quarterly: "Sway," "The Basho Doll"
The North Stone Review: "Saturday Bath," "Decoys," "An Elephant," "After Edvard Munch"
Passages North: "Beer," "The Tree of Rubber Tires," "The Common Expressions Our Grief Leads Us To"
Poetry East: "Chlorine," "A Little Poem About the Rain"
Poetry Northwest: "Air Guitar," "Think of Me in D Major," "On Summer Evenings Several Summers Before the Next War"
Prairie Schooner: "Friends," "Leftover Lines from an Old Journal," "Lemon Sun," "The Superstitions," "Work," "What I Did and What They Did About It When They Caught Me," "Richard Nixon," "Red Wine," "Gray Rain," "At the Mall," "A Bird Flies into the Room and Then Flies Out Again"
Salt Hill Journal: "Magic"
Sonora Review: "Fame," "The Building I Live in Is Tipping Over"
Virginia Quarterly Review: "Staff," "Stones That Seem To Have Grown from the Lawn," "Gladioli," "Pastoral"

"Staff" and "Another Word for Blue" were reprinted in *New American Poets of the 90s* (David R. Godine, 1991).
"Air Guitar," "Think of Me in D Major" and "On Summer Evenings Several Summers Before the Next War" were co-winners of the Helen Bullis Prize, *Poetry Northwest,* 1992.
"Friends" and other poems received the Strousse Award from *Prairie Schooner,* 1989.
"Fame" and "The Building I Live in Is Tipping Over" received a *Sonora Review* Poetry Award from *Sonora Review,* 1984.
"Fame" was reprinted in *Minnesota Writes: Poetry* (Milkweed Editions/Nodin Press, 1987) and in *The Decade Dance: A Celebration of Poems* (Sandhills Press, 1991).
"A Bird Flies into the Room and Then Flies Out Again," "Work," and "Think of Me in D Major" were reprinted in *Two Cities,* 1997.

Special thanks to The Bush Foundation for a Bush Artist Fellowship, to the Minnesota State Arts Board for a Creative Writing Fellowship, and to The Loft and the McKnight Foundation for a Loft-McKnight Writers Award, generous gifts that allowed me to complete this book.

CONTENTS

FOREWORDS

"Art means nothing feels safe as itself."
—*Letter from San Francisco to John Engman*

"The armless spud, no friend hath he."
—*Postcard from John Engman in Iowa City*

THE DEATH OF JOHN ENGMAN on December 10, 1996, at age 47, came as no surprise to the poems in *Temporary Help*, but it shocked anyone who knew him, especially those who had read his poems and chuckled knowingly at his comic premonitions of mortality. As a former teacher of his and older friend, I had always presumed that he would have to remember me, not me him. Once I called him wearily in the night and said, "Bad news, Johnny. You're going to have to write my poems for me. The good news is, I'm giving you all my metaphors." In such devious ways, I trumped his own poetic fatalism. But he had the ultimate say-so.

I don't remember when I first saw many people. But I distinctly remember the first time I saw John Engman. He had come to speak with the teacher with whom I shared an office at Augsburg College in the fall of 1968, my first year of living and teaching in Minneapolis as a Southerner in flight from my own sense of the absolute. John was a sophomore. He had come to make an inquiry about a response or lack of response to something he had written.

There he stood, "a blameless five-foot-eight," shifting his weight from foot to foot, with a quietude that was at once tentative, perplexed, urgent, annoyed. It was the inward intensity of the silence that caught my attention, his hesitancy at saying what was really on his mind, a fretful innocence or a perplexed naiveté that was wise beyond his years. I recognized that he was not satisfied by whatever had been said, that he wanted more, wanted something resolved for which the available answers were inadequate or absurd.

I don't remember how we became friends, but it had to do with poetry, with the way things are and the way we saw them. In my initial period of curiosity about him, a crucial insight occurred at a student party to which I had been invited. One of his friends remarked that when John had had a few beers he alternated between "uncontrollable sobbing" and "hysterical laughter." Later, when I first saw his poems, stark enigmas and comically free verse, I knew that he was precocious, not just a creative writing student, but a poet in the making. We moved closer to one another in the sublime and ridiculous enterprise that we merrily and scornfully called The Arth of Poesy.

.   .   .

Life goes on, and it gets serious. John Engman was not a person nor a poet whom one could easily put a finger on, much less lay a hand upon or put an arm around. Like most poets, he was extremely sensitive to his physical existence and psychic space. Despite the fondness people felt for him and the generosity of his own spirit, he often was self-bemused, strangely solitary, if ever alert and attentive to the human predicament of others. Certainly he did not like to be characterized, only experienced. Yet now, imagining posthumous protests, we must begin to speak of him and his poetry, aware that he resisted any authority over him and distrusted "all schools of thought," be they aesthetic, psychological, religious, professional, or social.

If we say he was hilarious, a very funny guy, we must also concede that he was dead serious, that he occasionally sobbed utterly, and that he could abruptly (if briefly and rarely) express anger or resentment. If he telephoned in the dark hours and melodramatically announced, "I hear your cries in the night, and I want you to know I am here for you . . . ," followed by a long exasperated sigh, we might well have supposed that it was his own cries that we ourselves had not heard and called to inquire about. If we presumed to share ourselves with him at a given moment's notice, we might well have discovered his preference to be alone.

If we claim that he was bedeviled by his cultural and economic predicament as poet and temporary employee with a Master of Fine Arts degree from the famous Iowa Writers' Workshop, we might remember that he was regularly, if perfunctorily, employed and that he made his ends meet. And we might consider the funeral gossip about the night when an unexpected visitor opened the door to his apartment and glimpsed him surreptitiously concealing a glossy magazine under the pillow of his chair. When an opportunity arose to sneak a peek, the visitor discovered *Money* magazine, not exactly a guide to the destitute.

In fact, there were acute distresses over time—frustrations and disappointments of a nature familiar to any poet. But always there was the reconciliation of the chuckle, the shrug, the retort. There was a period in the late 70s when John had bounced a few checks (due mostly to poor record keeping and always redeemed) at Lyle's, his neighborhood bar for twenty years. Howie, the short, busy, no-nonsense, balding but sideburned bartender from North Dakota, leaned on the counter, holding a frail piece of paper before John's face, and asked if this was another bad check? Composing himself with Laurelean nonchalance before Hardyesque pique, John replied, "Howie, there is no such thing as a bad check, only a troubled one." From that moment, the two of them began the sweetest of friendships, both dying within a year of each other, Howie from lung cancer, John from a congenital cerebral aneurysm, types of death John had so often and so eerily foreboded in his poems, as if he had some secret knowledge that only the art of poetry could apprehend and temporarily resolve.

As for his poetic sensibility, one would have to factor in such favored poets as Robert Frost, Dylan Thomas, Wallace Stevens, Weldon Kees, Frank O'Hara, and James Wright, not to mention Donald Duck, Buster Keaton, Laurel and Hardy, Elvis, Cat Stevens, Paul McCartney, the Salvation Army, the Rolling Stones, Tiny Tim, Jerry "Telethon" Lewis, the cast of *Cheers*, etc. As for clues to the heart of his vision, its ethics and consternation, one might well ponder the two works about magical children that I most associate with John's thematic perspective: Günther Grass's *The Tin Drum*, about a boy so shocked by the world at war that he refuses to grow up, to become a perpetrating adult, to speak—using his drum to protest atrocity; and Johnny Cash's gravel-throated rendition of "The Little Drummer Boy," about a boy who gives the only gift he has to the Christ child in the manger—his toy soldier's drum, which becomes the chosen gift. Or one might begin by reading "After Watching Korean Children Dying On Black & White Television, 1953."

What John did for a living, more consistently than any poet I have personally known, was read and write poetry—that was his drum, his guitar, his song, his gift, his end-all and be-all, all kidding aside. Ever wanting and needing more time to write was the source of his complaint about the occupational and interpersonal predicaments he found himself in, the constant dissipation of life-energy and life-time when the ordeal of poetry was so severe, its outcome so uncertain, and its joy so utter. Poetry, after all, might even help the world help itself—if only temporarily; at its best, it might please God, it might amuse friends and console strangers, it might redeem death—hence the wry humor and earnest endeavor of this collection's title.

At last, John Engman may be the healthiest, funniest, most tenderly consoling human being you will ever find between the lines of poems. Otherwise, you might note his art: the surprise of his metaphors, the urgent obliquity of his tones, his invigoration of the mundane, the humor of his self-appraisal, the modulation of his long lines, the sanctity of his concerns. If you do, then you will surely be able to think of him as one "swept away, but still here."

—John Mitchell

for John Mitchell

Just like one of us
the monkey folds its arms
in the autumn wind

—Basho

CREATION OF THE UNIVERSE

A tired angel
lugs a battered horn
up the steps of the cloud tower
but must rest on the escarpment
before awakening the sleepy molecules
with three weak blasts—for all I know,

it was like that.
Then Julia steps from number six,
on her way to the store for cigarettes,
and John crawls underneath his Rambler
to install new gaskets while David,
who hasn't yet suffered a cardiac,

tinkers with his ham radio,
still alive in number five.
Is Roger playing canasta in the basement?
Linda is up to her elbows in suds,
wondering if creatures live in outerspace
and what such creatures think of her,
who spends so much of an early evening
washing socks in the bathroom sink?
Rochelle and her guy have finally found heaven

and can't even hear the flutophone music
dripping like tears from number seven.
Anita roams the halls on rollerblades.
Greg has not arrived with three mad cats!
Margaret, gone uptown, and the evening calm:
I sit at my desk, as usual, writing a poem
as if working a puzzle, working a psalm. . .

Grace, in the kitchen of number three,
fans her stove with the old green rag
she wears in winter to keep the cold
away when she stays up late to talk
with friends who've gone before her to grave,
and watch the stars on Johnny Carson.
Her dinner of franks and red potatoes
has caught fire again, and her smoke alarm
can just be heard through the walls,
shrill and sweet as the lovesick
call of the cicada. . .

SATURDAY BATH

First, I undress.
Rising steam devours my physical being,
a peppermint fragrance from time-release
capsules of isopropyl sesquicarbonate, penta-
sodium triphosphate, Blue #7 and Yellow #3.
Perhaps I'm not the young Greek god I was,
but admire my body anyway, letting my mind
run wild with images suggested by the tub's
iron acanthus leaves and African lion claws.
Following my wet footprints across the hall,
you can find me drying with a cotton towel,
dousing with talc, strutting the future
ruins of my apartment, a misbegotten
ancestor, à la the amoeba.

"The human at his Saturday bath."
Imagine your afterlife captioned like that!
"Nights, he'd soak in noxious chemical powders.
Later, walking around half-naked was his habit:
swaggering, swaying his hips, imitating animals
he had put to death, until he felt 'beautiful,'
i.e., could be mistaken for wolf, puma, bull, elk.
This ritual continued every Saturday, a Saturday
the human calendar repeated, endlessly, without
cost. From his language come the archaic curses
Tin Lizzie, Bear Market, Endangered Species.
Of course, he is one of the lost."

GLADIOLI

Who thought your life would come to this?
Singing along with *The Greatest Hits* to a few
gladioli in a furnished room, Elvis in the suburbs.
What you were sure was a knock at the door
was only the radiator having spasms as the heat
kicked on. And you feel more alone than before,
feel your love for the whole world coming on

stronger than before, so murder this little tune.
You throw your head back and thrust your hips,
raising a fist the way the King did, as if lifting
a spirit. It's the way you felt riding a bicycle
home from the hell of school, doing wheelies, razor-
cuts and crazy 8s, until you felt dizzy and euphoric
as a true prophet. It isn't that you could love

everyone on earth with your small mind, but you do.
Only a song you heard on the radio in 1959 will do.
Dancing around like the King in your small room.
Millions of years of human evolution and you are still
you: sad astronaut, approaching the moon on foot.
You love everyone on earth, and they love you.
You croon in your room. And the gladioli nod.
Doo wappa. Doo wappa. Doo wappa doo.

GOLDFISH AT LORING POND

I'm standing with a sack of bread on the bridge at Loring Pond where the goldfish gather—they gape up at me with the vague and hopeful expression of distant relatives.

They must think that I am some spirit who has appeared to them this late afternoon in cold October, perhaps the ghost of Charles Loring, father of parks and bridges, father of calm, returning from the nineteenth century to feed them. They must wonder in their goldfish brains, who is this shadow who sprinkles the sky of our lazy pond with crumbs?

They make a golden cloud below me in the water, shadow of the golden cloud that is the elm that leans beside the pond, shadow of the golden cloud that is the sun going down into the city.

These shadows circle the middle of my life in late October, but I don't feel unhappy or alone, although the sky is gray and the sun is cold, and goldfish circle me as if I know—what?—that the sky is gray and the sun is cold.

I know goldfish, and can tell you, despite what experts say, that hundreds of goldfish are no more distinct than hundreds of flakes of falling snow. Although I may wait until winter to say so, wait by Loring Pond and have another look at the coming snow, at the pond swollen with snow, and the goldfish huge as pumpkins.

FAME

Putting a page into the old Royal
gives me a weird sensation, not much else.
One room below they must imagine I'm writing
the great American poem, something very smart
that only I know, but this is my fame: dark ages
measured by mineral rings from my drinking glass,
several pages weighed down with ink, one ration
of light that falls on pyramids built by spiders,
beds you can pull from the wall.

What can I write?
"It was a dark and stormy night and I was howling
in the skyhigh streets—Juanita, where are you!
My love will never die or will die in five minutes
without you, we must work fast. . ." Oh my.
Once upon a time my life was easier between lines
where the mind stays blank, nothing to confess
but this: everything I know seldom fills a whole page.
"Someday, I'll be dead." That was my idea.
"Someday, I'll be dead, Juanita."
That was my poem.

And someday my critics will know
this simplemindedness, and all this aloneness,
was my fame: how I show off my weaknesses,
a few cents' worth of dust and lost ingredients
who wants to make a good impression, like a leaf
in stone. So what if I stole my emotions: shyness
from the Murphy bed, ardor from the gooseneck lamp,
joy from the wooden chair? At least I let my poems
stay put until the last potluck, little sandwiches
Satan autographs with cheez-whiz. And someday,
Juanita, my fame will just be how useless
I am, beyond wanting and change,
"Baby, ain't no poems tonight,
just wind and rain."

BEER

Glaring down the bar, he announces
that he doesn't much care for the look of things
around here, and in my paranoid state, Minnesota,
I know exactly who he means. A poet, I fear anyone
who doesn't ignore me, and even as I drink my beer,
a rough face that moves closer by one stool scares me.
His eyes darken murderously, slashes between phrases
in poems Emily Dickinson begins with agony and ends
with flies and drills, welcomes and convulsions.

Fifteen stitches later, I think.
And then I can say I have suffered for my art.
Slurping beer, he tells me that he's read my poems.
"Maybe I'm old school, Bub, but that ain't real poetry.
I don't know how to sell out. Tell me how." He's surly.
But I tell him that I submitted a manuscript of my poems
to a panel of experts who judged submissions on the basis
of merit alone. I talk like that when I've been drinking.
"Bullshit," he tells me. "Government can't buy poetry,
no such thing. I mean rivers of darkness, mountains
of feeling. So much aching happens in true poems."

Then, from the bulge above his heart,
where I assume he's hidden a snub-nosed revolver,
he removes a volume embroidered with yellow tulips
and begins reading from the poems of Emily Dickinson.
Imagine the Amherst spinster trapped inside a small cow.
He reads for several minutes before he stops, abruptly,
and claps the book shut. Appraises me. Gulps his beer.
"I like a look of agony, Bub, we have a love affair."
Then he rises, crosses to a booth where he sits alone
beneath a small neon that says *Lite.* All afternoon
I buy him beer with money the government gave me
to write poetry. He doesn't speak to me again,
and I just watch: adorned by neon and sustained
by Dickinson and golden beer, one of those
recluse gods who seldom visit anymore.

ANOTHER WORD FOR BLUE

On better days, I bathe with Wallace Stevens: dreaming his good
    dreams before I fall asleep, waves lapping, none of the poorly
    choreographed crashing they do around here, but waves
    that can read music.
And one afternoon, when I felt a new dream studying me closely,
    I kept my eyes shut and lay flat, but the dream flew off,
    leaving me alone again, asleep with reruns.
People who don't understand what it means to be an artist
    should be punished, and I know how: make them be one.
Make them write about their own mortal souls in the third person,
    make them enroll at college, where they will be forced to write
    creative things about a piece of driftwood, forced to write
    poems about their moods using colors like "cerulean,"
    another word for blue.
People don't understand real artists: bottles with messages
    wash up on the beach, always a heartbeat ahead of the sea.
It isn't always a matter of being in the right place at the right
    time, wearing clothing that makes them notice you: black
    satin jackets and green string ties, crocodile shoes.
Sometimes it's a matter of being in the wrong place at the wrong
    time, unsinkable as Ivory Soap, an aesthetic theory
    that isn't much more than a plain bad attitude.
All I ever wanted was an ice-cold beer and a booth with a view
    of the local scene, that, and the adulation of multitudes.
There's a little place about a block from here where they never
    heard of free verse.

When they say they took a bath, they don't mean they spent
    an hour soaking with *Esthétique du Mal,* they mean
    they lost big bucks at the track.
For all they care, *Esthétique du Mal* could be bathsalts.
    They know two things: on planet earth "being yourself" doesn't
    mean much. And, there's no paycheck in pretending to be
    somebody else.
So when I tell the waitress, oh yeah, I could have been another
    Wallace Stevens—she tells me, oh yeah, so who needs two?
That's the kind of stuff that goes on in the poetry business.
And I am so pleased when I can refrain from expressing myself,
    refrain from saying anything new: I like saying the same
    old thing, words that stay put.
Words that don't go far, letting life remain a mystery for you.
Words I might say to a small group of friends someday, friends
    who will sponge me down whenever I begin raving about free
    verse back in the twentieth century, quoting at length
    from my own modest book of poems, a visionary work
    which sold poorly.

A BIRD FLIES INTO THE ROOM
AND THEN FLIES OUT AGAIN

Just as one of those simple people
who believe the world will end next Tuesday
drives through my neighborhood shouting "Repent!"
through a megaphone thrust from his black van,
I throw my window open for a gulp of winter air
and he begins shouting directly at me:
the government is falling and my brain
has been damaged by the blue light of television,
the last war is coming
and unless I do some quick work on my soul,
my stay in eternity will be mighty unpleasant.

He's crazy, but what he's saying is true:
scientists agree the earth is losing momentum,
that eventually the old 9-to-5 with two weeks vacation,
poor working slob at the wheel, kids in back with Ruffy,
Sally beside him, "sweetest li'l gal in the world,"
on their way to the lake for fishing,
will fall into the sun. Do I care?
I have no kids, no Sally, no Ruffy.
The room I rent is small and unpleasantly cold.
I don't even have a job—let it all fall into the sun!

I'm taking off my shirt now, unzipping my trousers,
climbing back on the bed to nurse my grudge
into fullblown depression when something stupid happens:
a bird flies into the room and then flies out again!
It scares me, the way that investigating angel
must have scared St. John when she came to judge,
grading him down for lack of grace and lack of lust,
"Dear John, you can do better. C plus, C plus."
So I'm standing here in my winter underwear
and my room feels cold but suddenly good—
if this is the way the world ends, that's okay,
it's winter, and my window is wide open.

THE WINDOW IN THE COW

You are a child with much to learn,
my professor said, when I compared
windows in cows to Nazi experiments.
The worst-case scenario for cows is veal,
he said, brief lives in small, dark stalls.
And didn't I eat steak? Someday I would be
dead, he said, of what might be diseases
cured by such cows. So I changed my thesis

and learned a first lesson in rhetoric:
try to think before you feel what you see.
From my dormitory room, I could see the cow
grazing pampered grasses, strolling her acre
of the University behind a chainlink fence,
scolding those who came to see her bowels,
and the four stomachs, with a woeful moo.
Like an Old Faithful or Mount Rushmore,

backdrops for photographs of children,
she was exotica for the family album.
And if she came close, mothers and fathers
could study her puzzling intestines through
glass held by rivets to her torso, encourage
the children, with oohs and ahhs, to step up
and rub her soft ears, the children amazed
that such a cow was willing to be touched.

RICHARD NIXON

Are you the President of pink flamingos and sad plastic flowers?
I remember you as a young man waving through a blizzard of television snow.
I remember you as an old man weeping real tears that fooled nobody.
I will do my best to remember you as a wise, china owl in a city garden.
Would you rather I remember you as a wise, china owl in a city garden
or as someone's father selling pencils in the rain under a streetlamp?
Do you believe America will fall to pink flamingos and sad plastic flowers?
I believe I could have been elected President but nobody voted for me!
The young woman sitting beside me on the bus could have been an angel
of Michelangelo but half her face had been destroyed by a grenade.

RED WINE

Something in his voice tonight
is like joy as he describes

red noise and *ribbons of white fire,*
the beauty of the bombing of Iraq.

We are watching a late broadcast,
a new war on CBS, and my friend,

a woman with whom I have not slept,
admires the way the anchorman uses

his voice to confuse sex and death.
Showbiz, I tell her, is great stuff.

But she says no, the human touch.
He warms our insides like red wine,

as if he rushed to the studio to say
folks are dying, the sky is falling,

just for us. We believe he is kind.
We believe he has never been kissed.

AFTER THE REVOLUTION

We're walking along
without a thought in our heads
when we just happen to look down
and see this stone in the middle of the road,
and we know the job has to be done,
so we elect this stone to be our President.

We all know those fields
that bring up stones
as if everything on earth
is seeking higher office—
too many candidates!

But our candidate
is all alone in the road,
cool and smooth and unblemished.
We fear he won't run!
Although he sits in the middle of the road
and says nothing
about the major issues of the day,
says nothing new or brave or realistic,
as if preparing for a long campaign.

We love him
because he seems so human,
warming up in sunlight and catching a chill in rain,
and gladly do we follow him,
which means standing in the middle of the road
until the road is overgrown, at last,
with weeds and wildflowers
and the political agenda
of the grass.

ON SUMMER EVENINGS SEVERAL
SUMMERS BEFORE THE NEXT WAR

The good boys said if you told
the psycho to eat dirt he would.
The big boys said be brave,
bounce rocks off his skinhead,
then run. The smart boys said
the evening wasn't safe,
the psycho lurking with his lizard claws
sharpened for small boys who tell mommy.
The small boys fled. And we boys stood,
exchanging dirty looks, the sky darkening.
Then some boy always said, "So what're
yuh made of? So what'll yuh give me?"

In this way we built legends large enough
for our ambition, although we didn't know
what our ambition was beyond sensation:
watching girls who sashayed home
from Dairy Queen at five o'clock,
detonating frogs with cherry bombs,
spit massaging Spalding gloves.
What fathers called the hunting instinct,
what mothers called young love,
what teachers condemned

as delinquent behavior,
drove us through the neighborhood,
a rotary storm, a gang of stumbles
and troubles. We loved all destruction.
And we loved baffling the adults—did God
make room in heaven for the souls of psychos?
Why did God make psychos? What did that prove?
And we loved the psycho, who helped us prove
what we were made of: playing by the junglegym
where we found sharp stones small enough
to bombard the kid from a safe distance,
who scared us with his unfixed eyes,
aviator's cap and green mittens.

STAFF

I got down on my knees with the little
weeds and whispered to them.
I counseled flowers, hey you, stand up straight.
I hypnotized a crêpe snake.
That's what I did for so many dollars an hour,
building a common garden of construction paper,
fingerpaint and scotchtape in the rec room
of the Adolescent Long-Term Treatment Program.

That garden was a cost-effective therapy,
and the dance we held that evening
was a learning lab, therapy disguised as fun.
The kids made funny costumes from bedsheets
and danced beneath stars of aluminum foil.
They played crazy music on the radio
and danced like crazy. Rock, funk, soul.
Anything can be therapy. And with lights low,
if that is allowed, any shadowy dance
can be a beautiful scene from a Hollywood movie.

I poured sugarless punch into styrofoam cups,
kept count of the dangerous plastic forks
and monitored touch. I stood back far enough
to translate body language, close enough to refeel
pain that might be used to document a diagnosis.

They were dancing like kids. Dancing like rabbits
behind wiremesh in the seclusion of a city garden.
Psychotic, arsonist, suicide—later, they'd suffer
the names life gave them. We tried everything.
And sometimes it was painful to watch them dance

with the skill they had to make dancing painful.
And when the dancing was done I uprooted the whole
garden, fashioned bouquets for the trash barrel
with fervor, like someone who needs psychiatric help.
Then dimmed the lights and sat in rec room darkness,
letting darkness fill me as an owl fills with wisdom,
a china owl in a city garden, waiting for something
human to happen and make sense, the patient approach.

AIR GUITAR

You bought television time with tokens,
stared at college sophomores cutting up
in dark costumes, playing air guitar.
They mouthed lyrics to loud music,
won prizes, acted young and dumb.
Age 13, you said they made you feel
thousands of years old,
and joked that they might respond
to behavior modification.

You did not respond to behavior modification.
Cutting your wrists, you made a dark costume
of dried blood that flaked from your arms
like sequins. We found you crouched
in the corner of your room, mouthing lyrics
in some sad song, strumming air guitar.

Perhaps he beat you. Unzipped, pants down.
And while your mother sat in the parlor
dreaming of Palm Beach and mahjongg,
did you like a dog. You hoped his love
was something you could forget soon,
couldn't wait to tell your brother,
who hid in the cellar, scissoring
crotches from panties of dolls.

Our knowledge of psychology enabled us
to make you feel dirty with a vacant stare,
and when you refused our request for anger,
we threatened you with isolation in your room,
as if your tenure as a patient were a failure.
We retold your tale to friends in bars.

The Diagnostic Statistical Manual of Psychiatric
Disorders defines your response as the bland,
maladaptive, Adolescent Adjustment Disorder
#309.28, of Mixed Emotional Style, loss
of feeling for the child inside you.
Doctors had fun with the question:
was there a child inside you?
They said there wasn't and there was.
Chemicals in the brain can reproduce
voices speaking from the abdomen:
a singer who says she loves you,
a singer who says she's cold,
a singer who advises you
to *cut something,*
cut something.

THE BASHO DOLL

That room
was the pink
experts say

helps people
stay calm.
The boy,

who claimed
he had fallen
from Saturn,

screamed curses,
banged his head
on the walls.

So much noise
in a room
anyone could fill

with a small sigh!
After an hour,
his face appeared

behind the 8x5
plexiglass shield,
perfectly calm.

"Basho was here,"
he told me, his captor.
"Basho, the Japanese

poet, came back
from the 17th century
to see me in this dumb

bastard hospital."
Then he recited poetry:
Broken, broken by shore,

waves so easily mend.

•

Basho sojourned
for years, knowing
bamboo by bamboo,

stone by stone.
Basho met strangers
and knew them, met poems

and knew them, drank
tea made from the rain
in his poems, knew

which images must go,
which images remain.
Stabilized, the boy

who fell from Saturn
wandered in his brain,
drank thorazine, saw

strangers everywhere
who spoke from clouds,
who spoke with howls,

who hounded him
and told his heart
to pound, or stop

if he refused to go
insane. He knew images
made pain, knew pain

encircled him like icy
particles from Saturn.
Basho gave him a poem

to help him see pain
clearly, as Basho saw
blossom in blossom,

stone in stone.

·

Suicide precautions
call for isolation
in a paper gown,

patients locked
in observation rooms
to keep them from harm.

He sat naked,
shredding his gown,
knotting legs, arms,

face and chubby torso
with threads of hair
pulled from his scalp,

creating a toy
from wads of yellow
tissue, a Basho doll.

Resting the doll
on his knee, a weary
traveler on a hill,

the boy would smile
and nod, listening
to what the doll said

the way children do
naturally, believing
dolls can talk.

Then, talking back,
softly, listening again,
as if to understand:

everything clear to him,
what Basho said, the way
dolls do, naturally,

in plain English.

ALUMINUM FOLDING CHAIRS

For three long years I ran group therapy
for three long hours times three sessions per long
week and no holidays twelve long months of each long year
long evening after evening and it made me kind of crazy.

I had no therapeutic degree,
but could say, "I hear what you're saying," without blinking
when someone touched his nose to my nose and said, soulfully,
"I can hear the bacteria in my yogurt singing."

What a therapist needs to succeed in group therapy:
a love for aluminum folding chairs and sad stories,
an aptitude for nodding your head and a strong desire
to scratch your stomach thoughtfully

while someone sitting beside you opens a wound
the size of a gymnasium. As I listened, I repeated this phrase
silently, automatically, inwardly, calmly, "I am immune
to the horrors of my own life." O Father of Psychoanalysis,

forgive me. I had no idea what I was doing.
I didn't understand the instruction book. At crucial moments,
I would earn my paycheck by leaning forward and saying,
"Look within yourself" or "I know where you're coming from"

or "Tell me how that makes you feel." After a few years,
when I realized that no one was listening, I began to improvise
with harmless asides like, "Keep your head down and swing
through the ball" or "Red sky at morning, sailors take warning"

or "Bake at 350 and cool before serving."
It occurred to me that I had lost my mind, but I told myself no,
that I had merely "mentally retired." I studied the patients
as they spoke, as the room became an aerodrome for ghosts,

and tried to hear what they were saying
but they seemed to forget stories even as they told them.
Their silence seemed a kind of praise for those who had survived
what they had spoken. They seemed to be waiting for something—

a moment of truth?
a moment of grace? a moment of healing? No.
They seemed to be waiting for the end of group therapy.
And when they stood and collapsed and put them away,

I heard what they hadn't been saying:
the clatter of aluminum folding chairs, the clatter of those
poorly-drawn birds that fly so often through children's stories,
mechanical but rising, awkward, but without lamentation, happy.

AFTER EDVARD MUNCH

Edvard Munch's *The Scream*
portrays a scream in oil paint.
The screamer is probably male,
although there is some confusion
and this helps disturb people—

worse, somehow, to imagine a scream
that comes from a male, hands raised
and head thrown back, than a female,
and the ambiguity aids the illusion,
making the horror more real.

Perhaps, waking from a bad dream,
the screamer is struggling to gauge
what is real and what is unreal,
as if he is suffering delusions.
Dreams make everything seem real,

and so he suffers and screams.
It's hard to determine his age,
but he certainly isn't aging well,
and so much screaming and confusion
can't help. Behind him, the people

seem distant, as if in a dream,
and the shrill hues of the landscape
aggravate, perhaps, until he feels
nothing but ugliness and frustration,
and nothing around him seems real.

Worse, somehow, if this isn't a dream,
but an illustration meant for all ages,
young and old, male and female:
the scream, not just an illustration,
unreal, but happening to real people.

MONEY

From a balcony at the Art Center
I can see everything, including a poor soul
whose life is his art, a dangerous type:
trampler of flowers and searcher for gold
from sunken armadas, mourner, sunset shouter,
apocalyptic pamphleteer. He sells pencils for 10¢,
all day tapping his white cane as if he's afraid
to fall from the edge of the earth, and then
at five o'clock, he removes his black goggles
and sashays home, enjoying the view, a fraud.

I watch him from the balcony,
sip my demitasse and play with the remains
of my croissant, the crusty part I never eat.
Time passes slowly in the upper atmosphere.
All day clouds blow around, making faces at me,
hello and goodbye, without sound. And down below
reality has run amuck: the blind can see,
as if a wire figure by Giacometti has suddenly
come to life, as if an illusion can only
go so far, and then turns back, things
being the way things really are.

SWAY

That horrible eyesore
was an ordinary citizen fifteen stories
before I wrote this poem. Nobody knows him.
Now he's data from a measuring tape, and dead,
a few wavy lines across a paramedic's notepad.
The morgue's van eases into evening traffic,
an earthworm traveling between the stars.

Facts, none.
A statement will be issued for the press
and one manilla folder will be stamped *Official
Business, Do Not Bend.* One life, one manilla folder.
The downtown people are familiar with these folders.
They help keep track by feeding all the sad details
into computer banks. The downtown people,

helpless without manilla folders
and a filing system, rubberstamp symbols
like the fingerpaintings done by prehistoric man
on walls of rock. One manilla folder, *Do Not Bend.*
File him under *S* for suicide from fifteen stories.
S for solid pavement. *S* for sad case of a citizen
who couldn't bend, who couldn't sway a single
blade of ordinary grass with one whole life.

THE TREE OF RUBBER TIRES

Following someone who's gone before
is what a mouse does, that's his career.
He noses around in the labyrinth for a bowl
of nuts and seeds, then goes back to the cage
where he is inconsolable, weeping soundlessly
in his nest of shredded tissue. On Saturdays,
he is almost human, running away from all his
troubles on a stationary wheel, putting miles
between himself and whatever he feels.

I run Lake of the Isles,
a labyrinth of charcoal grills and wild
geese, a chapel of Nikes and ten-speed bikes.
I run like a mouse, until an overwhelming sense
of ease replaces what I see: canoes and booming
sails, the city of Minneapolis, in silhouette,
and pets pulled around the lake by the neck.
That life holds no sad secret seems to be
the theme of Isles, what travelers

need, nothing to achieve,
a circular path. I circle Isles, circle
pans of burning coal, the sparks striking back.
Bikers take the sun on wobbly, inflatable wheels.
I run circles until I could have been many miles
from here, where travelers raise their children
behind a chainlink fence: blowouts and retreads
mounted on an upright pole, and little Tarzans
swinging from the tree of rubber tires.

THE LONGEST SIDEWALK IN THE WESTERN WORLD

Okay, unicorns exist. And scientists
say the palms of the hands became translucent
at the first Atomic blast. Someday, on the moon,
a human being will make very shallow footprints—
in outer space, everything from earth weighs less.
These are facts a traveling salesman shared with us
on our front porch in 1956. I remember little jars
of mint and menthol, atomizer sighs, soothing
balms for tricky wounds and tricky oils

to disguise the body's small flaws.
And how far prices fell if you let him talk
and talk! We sampled everything he couldn't sell.
"Friends, this is the land of the free and brave,"
he said, as my father scoffed, "What a snowjob."
And when it snowed, my father said that our block
had the longest sidewalk in the western world,
although not long enough to stop a salesman
who couldn't stop himself from an endless

life of talk. "When the sun rises,
you can see it nick the horizon, a green flash!"
We laughed and laughed, leaning back on the hind
legs of our wooden chairs, as if skidding to a halt.
And the salesman, raising his fallen argyle socks
before he stepped up the block, took the future
with him and his black valise of healing, sang
the poems of *Burma Shave* from house to house,
his baritone finally fading toward the edge
of town, the lakes and the graves.

WORK

I wanted to be a rain salesman,
because rain makes the flowers grow,
but because of certain diversions and exhaustions,
certain limitations and refusals and runnings low,
because of chills and pressures, shaky prisms, big blows,
and apes climbing down from banana trees, and dinosaurs
weeping openly by glacial shores, and sunlight warming
the backsides of Adam and Eve in Eden. . .
                                    I am paid
to make the screen of my computer glow, radioactive
leakage bearing the song of the smart money muse:
this little bleep went to market, this little clunk has none.

The woman who works the cubicle beside me has pretty knees
and smells of wild blossoms, but I am paid to work
my fingers up and down the keys, an almost sexy rhythm,
king of the chimpanzees picking fleas from his beloved.
I wanted to be a rain salesman, but that's a memory
I keep returning to my childhood for minor repairs:
the green sky cracking, then rain, and after,
those flowers growing faster than I can name them,
those flowers that fix me and make me stare.

I wanted to be a rain salesman,
carrying my satchel full of rain from door to door,
selling thunder, selling the way air feels after a downpour,
but there were no openings in the rain department,
and so they left me dying behind this desk—adding bleeps,
subtracting clunks—and I would give a bowl of wild blossoms,
some rain, and two shakes of my fist at the sky to be living.
Above my desk, lounging in a bed of brushstroke flowers,
a woman beckons from my cheap Modigliani print, and I know
by the way she gazes that she sees something beautiful
in me. She has green eyes. I am paid to ignore her.

THE COMMON EXPRESSIONS
OUR GRIEF LEADS US TO

I step into the classroom cautiously,
clearing my throat to let them know who I am,
a somewhat unwelcome professor who is welcomed
with looks of suspicion, last man on a crowded raft.
I grip the lectern with both hands. What can I say?
They wonder as I say them what my words want.
Some days, if I were paid to be honest, I'd say,
"Class, today I am having difficulty remembering
the names of the letters in the English alphabet.
And by the way, what class is this?" Trying to draw
an illustration of this circumstance in chalk, I fail,
erasing it quickly. I emit a series of nondescript snorts.

"Class, today we'll talk about how to resuscitate
a dead metaphor. You may ask yourself, why bother?
Is higher education really a punishment? But seriously. . ."
Already I have lost them. The front row glares
with that bewilderment freshmen usually save for fathers.
Some pretend to doze off, the smarter students ignore me.

Then I begin drawing diagrams in the air, waving my hands
as if flagging down a mirage. "The sea of life," I say,

"is a dead metaphor that suggests the darkness of the sea
will suck us down in our final hour, the deep six."
At the word *suck*, several heads rise from the desks.
Having caught their attention, I lean back, full of myself,
nibbling on my stub of chalk. Then, as happens so often
when I am in a philosophic frenzy, I square my jaw
and inhale deeply: crushing the chalk and swallowing
a lump that blocks my windpipe below the epiglottis,
gags me like exhaust from a passing freighter.
Grabbing myself by the throat, pausing

one second to reflect on how much real learning
happens by default, I choke and gasp for air. "Water,"
I whisper, and everyone laughs. One student, who scribbles
notes as I turn blue, lose my footing and grab at the air,
contributes, "That's not how you do the Australian crawl,"
and then, "Oh, sea of life, I get it." And the class applauds,
"Man overboard! Dead metaphor! King Neptune! Food for the fish!"
And as I crawl toward the door, they flutter above me, worried
as gulls by a man who throws signals instead of breadcrumbs.
And the voice that follows me into the hall is sure and swift
as the fin of a shark, "Will we be graded on this?"

WHAT I DID AND WHAT THEY DID
ABOUT IT WHEN THEY CAUGHT ME

I worked as an organ grinder's monkey or something, all I re-
member is showing up and doing as I was told by anyone who
approached me in a shop of some kind (or a church? a factory?).

There was pounding, sweeping and heavy lifting. There were
coconut-shell cocktails with little umbrellas stuck in them. There
were noisy machines with large gears in which you could lose an
arm. The insane screaming that began each eight a.m. gave me the
sensation that I was falling, and often I forgot who I was for as long
as an hour.

I would wake suddenly in this place, which I now believe was
some sort of cafe (or a hospital? a mortuary?) and realize that it
was I who was screaming, even as I pounded, swept or lifted heavy
things, whatever it was that I did.

The screaming seemed to be the service for which I was being
paid.

They said I was making good money. Who were they? But the
job didn't work out, so I quit, or they fired me, whatever—all of us,
we just let go.

All I know is that no one will pay you to sit around writing
poems all day, like a bum. You must go out and find yourself a
position doing something truly hateful for a low wage.

You must convince a total stranger that he should give you his
money because you have a special gift for flipping meat patties
with a spatula, for scraping dead bugs off windshields, for shovel-
ing gunk into little piles.

You must reassure this stranger that you are not some loath-
some character who enjoys flipping meat patties, scraping dead
bugs and shoveling gunk, but that you are, in fact, studying to
become a brain surgeon, an astronaut and a ballet dancer.

You must create the impression that although you feel his patties, bugs and gunk are beneath you, chances are that your surgeries, spacewalks and *grand jetés* will be flops, and you will probably flip, scrape and shovel for the rest of your life, gratefully.

All I know is that, finally, some loathsome character will be hired to flip, scrape and shovel what is left of me into the grave, and then everyone will go out for canapés and coconut-shell cocktails with little umbrellas stuck in them.

I just got fed up. And when the agent from the employment agency called, I told her that I found the idea of an honest day's work appalling, and that I was adverse to the common tasks of daily living, and that what might take me hours to accomplish, the less ambitious might finish in minutes, and that my hobbies included behaving like a lunatic in public laundromats: kneeling before the porthole of a pay-per-load-machine and shouting verses at the surf, remembering my homeland dear and the beautiful wench I left, the wind in my hair, the seas billowing.

The agent said, "Ah yes. We know your type. Your type is welcome here. Born, you did fine with diapers, pabulum, measles, acne, bicycles and girls. A Math teacher, sideburns curled like graying broccoli, drew charts on the chalkboard, serious signals you never understood. An English teacher, breasts as full as the first day of summer, beat you with her ruler. Then, the sensation of falling, black cap, black gown, as if attending the funeral of a clown. Your type hears the words of Dylan Thomas tumbling in suds of laundry. Your type feeds green dollars to the singing monkeys. Don't worry. You belong to this world. Please wear a tie."

Please wear a tie. That is what I did and what they did about it when they caught me. We are all dead. We are all living together in the basement of heaven, screaming and doing laundry: flipping patties, scraping bugs, shoveling gunk. They hired me. There is no human explanation for this.

SESTINA FROM THE NINTH DISTRICT

*The Federal Reserve Bank, suspended on two swaying
steel cables, is considered by some a masterwork of
art and architecture. But it's coming apart at the
seams. . .*

—Star Tribune, *1993*

    Our Federal Reserve Bank
floats in the air! It was a work of art
until the laws of nature took effect: asbestos
tears sprinkling from the ceiling as our supervisor
muttered about the money rehab would cost.

    Nowadays, art means money,
and no one knows this better than the Federal
Reserve Bank, or a supervisor whose supervisor rages
that so much work needs to be done, so many tears
shed because some artist denied the laws of nature.

    Imagination makes its own laws,
and anything seems possible if you have enough
money: if you don't mind suspending tons of tiers
of concrete from two thin cables to make a bank.
Just thinking something so crazy is hard work!

    And work done on your own, without a supervisor,
or with imagination as your supervisor, an urge to say,
"Forget natural laws, I want buildings to float in the air!
This will work!" But imagination must be fed with money
and you can't get money from a Federal Reserve Bank

that hasn't been built yet. Oh, the bitter tears!
And there is nothing in this world as useless as tears
when you talk to a bank officer, and then his supervisor,
and finally, you weep at the desk of the Bank President,
who is trying to explain that certain laws stipulate

no one as crazy as you deserves money,
even if your idea will work. But then he pauses, asks,
"Will this work?" And you notice that the Bank President
has splashed a few tears of his own on his shirt, and suddenly,
digging into his pocket, he gives you the money, saying,

"Don't tell my supervisor." Even a Bank President knows
the law of laws is money: you can't put imagination in the bank.
So you build the bank, but it doesn't work, demolished by laws
of the wind. And the supervisor who fires you says,
"On tears, that's where I put my money."

THE BUILDING I LIVE IN IS TIPPING OVER

The archaeologist who digs deep enough,
through the rock and rolling tiers of ape man
and ape woman, will find my lowly bones
just as I left them, in rows like a xylophone.
She may play my ribs with her rubber mallet,
reviving a mood from ages ago, the haunted
little tunes of my carbon 14 content.

This is what she will know:
I was a homo sapiens with few employable traits,
not much data for the data base: American male,
biped and carnivore, a blameless five-foot-eight.
Perhaps she'll bring me home in a canvas sack
and stash my remains in a storage vault
as if she's collecting antiques. . .

I may be worth money someday!
My skeleton, the backbone of some new dream!
I doubt that, but imagine how pleased she'll be,
digging through the stream-of-consciousness rock
until she arrives at my flat, and petrified me,
caught in the act of whispering sweet nothings
through the fossil of a keyhole. . .

LEFTOVER LINES FROM AN OLD JOURNAL

I remember sitting on a gray, wicker chair
while someone pretty whittled my likeness
from a russet potato. I remember toying
with her hair, and later, her hands
calling Brahms from the piano. I remember

wondering how we remember who we are
and who we are not each morning
when we awaken, startled from bed
by the alarm, as if pelted with shot.

I remember remembering this in December,
cold where I was hidden with my secret
thoughts near one street named for a tree
and one street named for a river.
I was waiting for someone who came so late
that what I meant to say was lost
until I saw her in my thoughts

thirty years later at a bus terminal.
She's still pretty, I wrote in my journal.
I remember writing that sentence again
and again, like practicing scales
on a childhood piano, and can't remember

why I let the sentence end, can't remember
what she saw in me beyond my eyes,
the eyes of a russet potato. I remember
saving grasshoppers in jars for her,

remember my funhouse face in the mirror
of the bowl of a spoon she hung
from her nose to be dear.

How lilac fumes made night a funeral parlor.

I remember wondering what God would do
if he missed her, sitting alone
with his terrible stars.
And that must be why I have written this
for her, as if she cares, to remember
my remembering: pianos and potatoes,
spoons and mirrors, lilacs,
and toy hair.

SOBBING UNCONTROLLABLY IN PUBLIC PLACES

That was the very room that we made
famous with our love, where our souls flew,
crying out and sighing. And that was the room
in which I wrote about her in my dreamy logbook,
thinking a few pages of blue ink would do the trick.
That was the very room in which, the wonder of love
is how I put it, the wonder of love and I succumbed
to the laws of physics and all of her beautiful moves.
"Well, you're sure nobody I would pick from a crowd,"
is how she put it, and gave me a look that ate me
slowly as a poem, no wondering allowed.

And blah, blah, blah.
Thankfully, I will never be one of those
who expect too much from a poem, who want the poet
to explode before he goes, leaving the rostrum draped
with glitz. Thankfully, I will never kill time by striking
a pose: malcontent who dreams too much, sullen fugitive
beneath the amber lamps, prince from a fallen regime.
And I don't have to go around sobbing uncontrollably
in public places to get my point across—that is
for those who want cheap thrills and headaches,
the personal touch. Let them read prose.

Of course, any young poet
should be able to describe a room,
a few pages of blue ink in a spiral notebook.
Any young poet should be able to describe a room
so poignantly it makes your eyes wet and you continue
reading with heavy sighs. But remember, there was a girl
on the bed, and we were in love, and the room was dark—
I really wasn't a poet yet. Sure, there should have been
a villanelle in her every move, her every look another
blank page torn from the moon, but my mind had a hole
worn through it by her touch, and the funny thing is,
I don't remember much. Oh love, you crack me up.

AN ELEPHANT

I abandoned Sharon first.
Sharon claims she abandoned me.
The dog abandoned both of us,
and wherever he went, stays put.
It's awfully hard to talk about,
but I still love her, madly.
In my dreams, or so she says,
she pats the dog. Maybe the dog
dreams we're together again,
sitting around admiring the dog.

His name was Shep.
Although I often called him
Sharon when I was adrift
on the barren island of desire,
where even Sharon could have been
good company, the Sharon I left,
who often called me Shep.
Although she would never admit
what she said, she will admit
she can't remember what she said,
and that was the whole problem

with our relationship: Shep.
The dog was our family secret.
Me, calling Shep by Sharon,
and Sharon, calling me by Shep.
It's awfully hard to talk about,
but the day I left, the day before
Sharon claims that she left me,
Shep called it quits and left us.
No one can build a relationship
on just the memory of a dog.

Sharon says she loved me
but the dog came between us.
Then she says, turns around
and says, we were never in love,
but that she still loves Shep.
I love tragedy as much as anyone,
but not being in one with a dog.
Sharon, you know I will never forget,
and someday I hope that you
will remember all three of us, fondly.
Shep, you know I will never forget
those nights you sat by the bed,
making eyes at us while we made love.
And Shep will never forget us, I know.
That dog had a memory like an elephant.

A LITTLE POEM ABOUT THE RAIN

There is a chance of rain on Minnehaha Avenue.
That's how a poem should start. But they won't pay
for little poems about the rain—they want "art."
Why didn't you take notes at the poetry workshop?
Don't say you drove the lonely avenues of rain.
Don't say rain whispered harsh words to the moon.
Don't say someone you love has left you nothing
to say but the moon on lonely avenues of rain.
Just put words on paper quickly as the hummingbirds
done by God. Then be happy, you have written a poem.
And maybe you are alone, but it's early, maybe someone
driving through a chance of rain on Minnehaha Avenue
is thinking of you as she sways through a curve, shudders
into the straightaway and pulls over: killing the engine,
closing her eyes, weeping aloud on the soft shoulder.

CLOUDS ABOVE THE BASILICA

Why was I telling the black dog about Marla?
Marla knew everything, I said. The black dog splashed
the asphalt with drool, as if stunned by such a thought.
Wind and leaves clattered in the eaves of the Basilica.

Marla could read black dogs
the way psychiatrists read crackpots,
the way gypsies read the past in an upturned paw,
the way old soldiers read the future in old newspapers.
Marla couldn't be fooled by a black dog, I said.
The black dog gave me a woof and a look,
a child whose nose has been rubbed
for wisdom in garlic.

We're in a funk at Lake and Lagoon.
We're in a funk at Seven Corners. We're in a funk
at Lyle's, Caesar's, Loring Bar, but later, huddled
by the pond, refusing goons and midnight cruisers,
me and Marla thumbing whatnots at the stars.

Later, it's Marla drawing lipstick lashes
on the headlights of a Porsche, Marla doing the sofa dance,
surging at Cafe Nada, Marla singing sweetly from our balcony
at three a.m., an aria, the black dog adding his alto
as my Marla showers him with our last champagne.

Where was Marla?
Such things are difficult to explain to a black dog,
a black dog steaming and trembling, a black dog slobbering
as if I am St. Francis of Assisi visiting his rundown neighborhood
of mammal bones, aristocratic cats and rubber balls. Clouds
quarreled above the Basilica, and the black dog glared, as if to say,
just tell the truth in black dog language, which I couldn't do.

We don't know who we will be when we get there,
Marla said, about the past, as if she assumed that everyone knew
we were living backwards. People were leaving the Basilica fast,
and traffic crawled under sudden thunder, then rain, at last.

The rain kept me talking.
1973 took hours. Rain was playing me like a piano. The black dog,
who didn't have a clue, kept pushing his cold nose into my crotch,
asking where has Marla gone? An aria echoed from the apse of the
    Basilica.
Then, as if in answer to this new world my wanting Marla had made,
my first tears fell like black dog slobber, recycled champagne.

TERRIBLE WEATHER CONDITIONS

Am I poor?
Are the leaves falling because I can't afford them?
Am I crazy? I think the leaves are falling because I can't afford them.
Am I alone? Autumn leaves are falling like little lessons

but I haven't learned anything.
The wind is cold and the leaves have fallen for three days.
For three days, the leaves illustrate how your hair falls.
Wouldn't you call these terrible weather conditions?

Loud sky, red rain, white crow, moon flying away.
How can I love you in autumn when everything goes wrong?
Last night, I burned three hundred calories dreaming about your hair.
I thought I felt animal earth lurch forward

and fell into the dark ages between now and now.
Sometimes, I want you to believe that I am an ancient poet
who can say grand things, "Last night, I couldn't sleep
because the leaves were having an excellent

discussion full of sad knowledge." But really,
this is sweet confusion, mistaking leaves for something more,
and all I can think to say is, "Do you like leaves falling?
I would like to see you today. That's all."

Someday, what will I be when I am nothing but a flutter
behind your breastbone like a leaf falling? Will you be the sky?
Wouldn't you call these terrible weather conditions? There's a hole
in the bottom of my old brown shoe, a hole in the sleeve

of my old gray coat, a hole in the pocket of my old blue shirt
where the wind blows autumn in and chills me: wouldn't you call these
terrible weather conditions? Something should be done about this.
Someone should write to someone, as I am writing to you.

CHLORINE

In the shallow end,
where I can stand,
I let the water

chill me slowly,
pull on skull cap
and plastic goggles.

I check my pulse.
Then do laps,
one lap for each year

of my life on earth,
a long mile back
to the year of my birth.

I swim by the house
where I grew up.
I swim by my father

and mother and sister
and gramps. The little
blonde boy who waves

is me. At the deep end,
I flip and turn back,
circle like a thought

through the overbearing
blue that children use
to portray the sky.

Then nothing left of me
but blue and the smell
of chlorine, flowers

plucked from the tomb
of an ancient King
who died young.

LEMON SUN

I help them escape my Royal,
pumping the black keys. My father,
who wants to see the manager, who wants
his say, "How would you like it? Forty
years cooped up in a boy's right brain!"
My mother, who isn't afraid of poetry,
who is afraid I won't say much, and so
won't get paid, "This poem you wrote,
which end goes up?" And the poem

hurries across the page,
wanting much more than them in it,
layers of meaning and shadows galore.
But my mother pours my father a cup of tea,
and nothing unexpected happens: a breeze
blows through, the creak of a screen door.
And my big cathedral Royal rattles on,
letting half of me that feels crazy
speak for half that feels alone.

Everyone knows a poem
that can't beat death isn't art,
but a thousand iambs and a dash of euphony
cannot express much more than my mother
and my father, hiding smiles in cups of tea:
bitterness eclipsed by twists of lemon, kitchen
chairs in lemon sun. How this poem loves them!
Says so, plainly. And where they live all
shadows should be ashamed, all clouds,
and all things difficult to name.

MAGIC

A dimestore magic trick
my father loved was the magic thumb,
a pink shell painted with the moon of a human nail
where a hankie could be hidden,
and with my father's thumb concealed inside the magic thumb,
the illusion was that he had come empty-handed
and to prove he was a good magician
would pull something from thin air.

I knew he kept the magic thumb in his junk drawer,
knew he had plucked the diaphanous pigeon
of a white hankie from my mother's linen,
knew he had spent several minutes
fumbling to ball and stuff the hankie into the thumb,
knew he had palmed the thumb, knew he wanted to appear
nonchalant and that I should applaud
as if he were mysterious.

What I thought was mysterious
was not his magic but the magic thumb,
how easily inches of my father could disappear,
his thumb, the stuff he was made of, suddenly vanishing.
The dimestore thumb, not warm to the touch,
discarded in his junk drawer when the magic was done.
Which is not to say that my father was a bad magician

and that I am a bad magician's son,
but merely that it took him several years to learn
to reverse such disappearances, an anti-vanishing act,
to learn to conceal my own small thumb as if I were young
but vanishing quickly, a boy he could pull from thin air—
suddenly he'd lift the magic thumb and sweep the room
with his good strong arm, announcing it like magic,
"Look who's here! Ladies and gentlemen, my son."

WHAT I REMEMBER OF WHAT THEY TOLD ME

Introducing herself as Evelyn,
my mother, one of several dozen local beauties
whose audition for the lead in *Panther Woman* flops,
recites a limerick beneath the burning kliegs,
bats her eyes at the dark upper Orpheum, keeps time
to the redhot pulse of a balding Broadway scout's
cheroot. This is how she knew it would be

in her dreams, but when the dramaturg
blurts, "Miss Olsen, please speak up. And smile,"
Evelyn raises her voice and gets the punchline
wrong by a mile. Meanwhile, somewhere in Michigan,
Robert, my father, is falling from a tall tree.
One small state and several thousand birdsongs
away, he is falling through what will become

his favorite history, a lesson
he'll repeat while trying to explain how accident
is destiny, how fact responds to memory, when he meets
Evelyn in fifteen years on Minnehaha Avenue. They'll marry.
But first, he must fall from this tree, breaking his arm.
Daughter of Einar and Johanna, son of Theodore Isadore
and Esther, they're just too young to wonder

what life means beyond summer
and the bombshell sun, beyond winter, what must be done.
They're just the right age to discover pain and pleasure
give a double meaning to the history of seeing stars.
It's the year Evelyn's voice cracks. Robert's elbow snaps.
A year they will remind each other of in years to come,
and ask, would you live that again, without regret?

And the answer is yes, although
they don't know that yet, because they are trapped
in antique darkness, seeing stars. Because they are young
and alone, have never met. Because Evelyn is about to learn
she will not be a heartthrob. And Robert, that he is doomed
to fly without wings, just human arms. Everything, a mess.
Just history, and what life means is anybody's guess.

AFTER WATCHING KOREAN CHILDREN DYING ON BLACK & WHITE TELEVISION, 1953

I couldn't sleep in my old room
unless I was buried by heavy blankets that kept my face
hidden from the red animals who came after me in bad dreams.
And I was always running, always running but always waking
where I had begun—in my old room with wolves and crocodiles
stalking me, animals with human features, carnivorous decals
from Walt Disney cartoons. As a child, I mourned my white
animals and mourned life at home:

the broom, the oatmeal ration,
forsythia in crystal, Bible in the bathroom, squeezebulbs
of perfume. I meant to conquer the unknown world beyond
our paisley davenport, beyond the lonely chiffonier, mammoth
brass lamp's ugliness, bearclaw Duncan Phyfe and baby grand.
Sometimes, I just sat in the dark, watching the shadows grow
terrible, waiting for the next moment to happen, mourning
a future I guessed was becoming, minute by minute
less and less. There were

long nights on a kitchen chair, my skin
cooling in the moonlight that poured from our Frigidaire.
One wall away my mother and father, strangers who belonged to me,
slept in secret little whisperings of body heat. Sometimes I watched,
pictured my blue animals entering their dreams, chasing me down.
Then I went back to my room, where I fooled myself into thinking
no time had passed—by feeling with my hand for the exact
posture I'd been sleeping in, still warm, a life-size
depression in the cotton mattress.

DECOYS

The lone drake
who startles us seems to be daring us
to follow, coming in low and setting his wings,
then turning toward the larger bay while we fire
at air. The drake disappears, calling his song

from a low cloud. My father fiddles
with the five-horse, checks the throttle,
chokes and pulls. His motions rock the boat,
making waves from our blind by the island.
The five-horse sputters, then floods,

and we breathe sweet gasoline.
Gasoline rainbows the bay as my father frees
the prop from a snarl of weeds. He chokes and pulls
while I row, gathering our dozen rubber mallards,
three cork geese, stuffing the gunny sack

after I wrap with anchor string
the arc of the neck, the detail of the wings.
The oars crackle as I pull them through the water
where the shallows have begun to ice and shine.
The last of the sun burns in the high reeds.

We are going home.
My father opens the throttle, chokes and pulls,
chokes and pulls. Then, because the moment pleases us,
we drift, as if there were no more to it than this,
the getting of wisdom, a day ending on open water.

THE SUPERSTITIONS

—for my mother

The switchbacks
help me rise
slowly on both feet

into the blue,
rather than crawl
on hands and knees

up the steep
Superstitions.
I stop and look back

into the rare green,
breathing cold drafts
of sweet lupine

and stinky creosote
that rush up the arroyos.
April on a canyon trail

of loose stone
that could throw you
into hypodermic ocotillo,

ardent cholla: a path
to the sky, crisscrossed
by skinks. Rose, peach

and lavender desert mallow.
Night-blooming cereus.
The giant saguaro.

Every living thing,
a small refusal: and no
surprise a deep purple

daring from the barrel
cactus, violent yellow
blossoms that erupt

like noise from paloverde.
After a winter of harsh
patience, sudden flowering.

And visitors like me,
who love desert flowers
cautiously, walk slowly,

and shy from spines
of prickly pear, calico,
holycross and fishhook.

Here in the Superstitions,
where we believe what grows
should be discouraged

by the tedium of sun on sand
and sun on stone, what grows
is ravishing and cutthroat.

And as high as I can climb,
dust devils stalled below,
the giant saguaro looms

from the canyon wall,
huge arms raised
as if carrying

blue from the sky
to some more final
rest, a gesture

any human audience
can recognize
as praise.

AT THE MALL

The astronauts seduced me
with smiles they had brought with them from Earth,
floating around in a space capsule
on several dozen color televisions
which were on sale.

I've never seen so many astronauts!
I've never seen so many color televisions!

There were more astronauts and color televisions
than shoppers shopping for new, color televisions
and that made me sad—all the mall
shoppers seemed sad, and the astronauts,
dogpaddling in weightlessness, seemed so happy.

It made me want to buy a color television!

I thought those smiling astronauts might console me
if I brought them home and tried to float around
in space myself, practiced a little joy,
more easily accomplished with a new, color television!
So I bought a new, color television.

I already have two color televisions at home!
And when I finally turned on my new, color television,
the astronauts had floated away and been replaced
by another smiling face who was saying sadness
could be erased by a certain kind of deodorant,
the way the wind can make it seem that someone
you can't see is walking through a field of flowers.

PASTORAL

James Wright, 1927-1980

On one long road from here
I spent the time with some of those
you have heard of, who gave up our town.
They introduced me to much more of the sky
I had missed, and to the only cow of the farm.
By some enchanted circumstance I was meant
to make friends. So I asked the big white nose
as much as I knew about the business of milk.
The cow stood. Things were not going good.

So then, I will tell this mammal
about myself, and the milk I give, which is
in my enthusiasm and business of human poetry.
Not a lick. So what I thought, I shall instruct
this cow in the ways of the beautiful green hour
a shadow can become in the James Wright poem
of the farm where he lay in an island of pine.
Of interest maybe, the ravine and brethren
of said cow wandering through the poem,

vanishing into the late afternoon.
It was so human, I said. It fit this world.
And taking a serious look into eyes of a cow,
I know now that every mortal word you can say
becomes confession, what I learned on the farm.
The eyes are deep blue so you remember heaven.
The cow is big and brown so you remember how
cow listens when there's nothing else to do.
Chews cud. Shares a long and elegiac moo.

STONES THAT SEEM TO HAVE
GROWN FROM THE LAWN

Maybe what I wanted was all wrong.
I hate to speak against what I know
has gone on for thousands of years
in the human animal kingdom.
I hate to speak against
tradition, names and slogans
chiseled into rows of stones.

I hate to speak against acres of holes,
and what we lower into darkness
wearing Sunday clothes.
Perhaps I should be satisfied
with what the sunlight shows:
vines on iron fences, shadowy cedars
hiding the graves of people I used to know.
Maybe I should just watch from the road.

I know it's green there, and people hired
to mow, sprinkle and take care are kind,
will kindly tell me which walk
winds down to someone I was sorry had to go.
They mow and sprinkle with such care,
the way an artist grooms a dream in pen and ink.
Maybe what I wanted I wanted
because I didn't know how to behave
in a quiet room with walls made of small breezes,
and maybe that was wrong.
I hate to speak against fat blossoms in glass jars,
and what else would you bring?

I hate to speak against marching the aisles
between stones that seem to have grown
from the lawn, saying the names of strangers,
saying the names of friends.
I hate to speak against enjoying the flowers
and feeling the sun on my face.
I hate to speak against anything that lets me enter
and then enters me, the way flowers move
slowly in the sun, making adjustments.
As if I could move slowly as a flower.
Maybe I should have wanted that.

FRIENDS

Now there is no getting you back.
Tom, who crashed. Lona, of cancer. John,
of the heart. Thanks to each of you for my share
of falling apart, if grieving is falling apart,
if writing is grieving. I spent time at my desk.
But now that you are dead I will write a poem for you
is a poor excuse only a poet would use, and poetry
is words you can't forget, words said to friends,
who forget them for you.

Well, it's sad.
I know a poet is supposed to make people feel more,
but I made people nervous with the things I said.
On Loneliness, I wrote a poem about my sperm,
"You should meet a nice egg and make something
of yourself." On Wordlessness, a poem about
a poem, "Just look at the lines experience
has drawn on my face with a blunt crayon."
Metaphysical stuff like that.

But your three lives
escaped me, and I knew you, and I knew you
wouldn't just come crawling back into any old poem
but would enter shouting whoo, whoo, whoo! the way
someone who is loved and unexpected enters a room.
And all I would have to say is *welcome.* Welcome.
Here you are in this poem that I wrote for you,
this ruined contraption where I should display
a whole range of emotions on a single page,
but I can't. I let them pass. So memories

are disobedient like children
whose impossible demands I can't answer
without words. Although I know someone who can:
the artist who draws a silhouette around the body
of another human being whose breathing has stopped.
Curious fact: the body makes an X of pure white chalk
but the soul makes none. One of those little mysteries
that I can't explain. All I can say is, give thanks.
And let them pass. Or, a poem might begin,
"They were very beautiful. I saved three of them.
I wish I knew what they were."

THINK OF ME IN D MAJOR

I know everything I know about dying
    (all doctors do
    is hope and cut)
from what I've been told by my own soft brain
while waiting in a waiting room:
              "Dying

seems to be something living organisms
    do naturally.
    You might be next."
I'm waiting for a doctor to check my pulse
and draw blood. I feel sick, not dying,
             but scared,

and poor Johann Sebastian Bach is trying
    to comfort me
    in D Major,
soothing with high strings, then coming in low
for a few notes, as if to say,
             gravely,

"Maybe you think about dying too much.
    Why, even you
    could live and be
swept away by a dose of baroque music."
The doctor who examines me agrees
           with Bach,

reducing all my intimations of mortality
    to medical facts,
    psychosomatic
muscle spasms and gas pains. I am alive,
but the prognosis isn't good: someday I will
        be dead,

and even the doctor admits that he can't find
    one cell
    of my soul
with his silver instruments and microscopes.
It's hard to believe that anyone can live
        hopefully

if the body is simply a score written in red
    and white counts,
    brainwaves, x-rays.
But harder to believe that anyone can die
when Johann Sebastian Bach argues
        for the soul

in D Major, a symphony of goosebumps.
    Maybe what dying
    organisms call
living is learning how to be swept away?
I admit that I feel swept away, somewhat
        immortal,

with Johann Sebastian Bach in the air.
    So, if someday
    I disappear,
just think of me as a goosebump, or a note
that disappears in D Major, swept away,
                but still here.

TEMPORARY HELP

After the actor who portrays me
in my dreams dies in my sleep,
dawn, I wake and climb from bed,
poor impersonation of the real me.

So this is what separates
man from beast, the nerve to say,
"I don't feel like myself today."

Today, I feel like a plebe in the army
of grassblades, the navy of stones.
Today, I feel like the spirit children
of Atlantis prayed to, father of ghosts.

Today, I sit me down with a cup
of granulated instant and count blessings:
my face, my arms and legs, my 26 teeth.

And through the walls I can hear people
killing people on TV. The anchor drags,
his words rising and falling like dying
notes in a Bach fugue. *Bodies*, he says,
are piling up. Nobody knows what to do.

Sometimes life doesn't want to be a dream,
as when an amber necklace worn by the moon
becomes, at dawn, just mercury-vapor lamps.

At dawn, the moon stalls in my window,
as if waiting for encouragement.
I can understand the moon.
The moon wants to influence world events
but keeps attracting seawater and local
folks who claim to be the lost Czar.
Bodies are piling up, I tell the moon,
and that should help you understand:
I'm having an identity crisis,
I finally know who I am.

    •

I'm waiting for the bus
and that mattress of gas, the sky,
is making me feel blah and unwelcome.
Another Monday morning and I'm working someplace I hate,
making money for someone I don't know,
adding to the gross national product of woe.
The bus is late. The clouds are low.

This is not literature,
this is my life and Monday morning,
what people who don't read books
call "really true." Getting through the day
is what I worry, how to avoid
becoming a story for the morning news:
not to be run down by traffic during rush hour,
not to be eaten by cancer from chemicals in fatty foods,

not to drown in my computer's beautiful
cathode ray blue. I'm worrying. That's what I'm doing
when a red balloon comes drifting up the avenue,
surrendered by the sky, dipping and swooning,
dangling a string. It's 7:30 in the morning
and I'm in no good mood for the gloom

to be lifted by the blush of a red balloon.
I'm suffering from depression in a bus shelter,
feeling wounded at the crossing of two avenues
no one will have heard of in a thousand years,
feeling sorry for myself, feeling round-shouldered,
inhaling exhaust fumes. Still, something
a red balloon can bring against the gloom
seems really true, floating from nowhere
to the roof of a bus shelter.
I jump for the string.

.

I take the elevator up,
follow arrows wing to wing,
find my name on the cubicle plaque.
I work in a giant building:
forty floors and forty cubicles
per wing, four wings per floor,
one person and one personal
computer per cubicle, a labyrinth
in which everyone's goal is to stay lost.

Although I must work here until the end
of the day, I can let my mind drift.
I can gaze from my high window
to the edge of the city,
houses where thousands of people
I will never know will always live,
and beyond, beautiful but alarming,
the curve of the earth as it turns
through what another solar system's
citizens must call outer space.

It makes me feel important,
thankful to my molecules for being me,
my DNA chain gang working another day
so that I don't suddenly become vapor.
If I can be someone forever,
let me be who I am while gazing from this window,
from this third planet in our local galaxy,
between Mars and Venus, five million years old.

These moments that could change me
forever don't come often enough
and when they come I don't often see,
although I remain alert and curious
as I work at my desk this morning,
this moment at the end of a century,
this hole in the day through which I fall
with earth as it falls through the sky,
the current universe before my eyes.

GRAY RAIN

The rain falls with you in mind.
But when the rain stops and the clouds break,
letting in a little sunshine
dedicated to the memory of Vladimir Mayakovsky,
bluebirds in the trees begin singing,
"Who is Vladimir Mayakovsky?"

You want to run out and yell into the trees
that he was a famous Russian poet who was persecuted
for harmless ideas, like poetry and peace,
but somebody would complain,
somebody call the police.

You are no Vladimir Mayakovsky!
You are a man who works downtown,
who wears a dark tie and white shirt.
Are there too many ideas like you in the universe?
Are all these tall buildings
obsessed with the same thought—
man in dark tie and white shirt,
man in dark tie and white shirt,
man in dark tie and white shirt?
Are all these tall buildings no smarter
than trees which keep repeating—
sway in the breeze, drop leaves, grow them back,
sway in the breeze, drop leaves, grow them back?

You are no Vladimir Mayakovsky
but you have been fruitful and multiplied
and made a general mess of things
although you believe that Earth will survive:
you hope to save mountains,
hope to save prairies,
hope to save seas.

You hope bluebirds will not be persecuted for their beliefs:
they should be allowed to live and keep singing.

You sit quietly at a small desk
in a dark tie and white shirt.
Vladimir Mayakovsky wore a blue beret
and in 1930 he blew his brains out,
leaving behind an unfinished poem
and the blue beret.
When the rain begins to fall again
it falls with you in mind but bluebirds
keep singing to no one in particular,
"Who is Vladimir Mayakovsky?"

ROCK FORMATIONS, CYDONIA, MARS

> *. . . old photos showed what might be pyramids, a*
> *fortress and other artificial designs on the rocky, red-*
> *hued plains of the Cydonia region of Mars. Indeed,*
> *the photographic lore of Mars since two Vikings*
> *visited the planet in 1976 includes faces alleged to*
> *look like Senator Edward Kennedy, a gorilla and*
> *Kermit the Frog. . .*
> —Charles McDowell
> Richmond Times-Dispatch, *1993*

One billion dollars for a ticket
to Cydonia, and the trip was long, but we had a mission:
to travel the dark and learn what we could from Mars
about life on Earth. We returned with photographs
of a gorilla, Kermit the Frog and Ted Kennedy.

They seemed to be the work of intelligent beings,
if intelligent beings would build monuments of red rock
in the uninviting plains of Cydonia. They were huge as pyramids.
Did Martians really know gorillas, Kermit the Frog and Ted Kennedy?
Was their mission to commemorate what they had seen on Earth

or were they just fooling around in the dark?
We have better things to do on Earth, even if they don't in Cydonia.
We have a mission. We have gorillas, Kermit the Frog and Ted Kennedy.
In the beginning, gorillas. Then slow evolution, from miniature frogs
to huge Ted Kennedies, our mission: to become intelligent beings.

So we shot a rocket from Earth and photographed
rock formations we mistook for gorillas, Kermit the Frog and Ted Kennedy.
(Cydonia was dark and we are not always intelligent beings.) Our mission,
our *real* mission, was to become as intelligent as our genes would allow,
to evolve beyond gorillas, Kermit the Frog and Ted Kennedy,

    another small step into the psyche's dark.
Cydonia was just a stop on our flight to the heart of the Earth.
We were dark missionaries, unintelligent beings in a space bucket,
malcontents in orbit. What did we find in Cydonia? What we found
was a gorilla, Kermit the Frog and Ted Kennedy. Nothing but us.

EARLY POETRY

It was in the time before we had thought up the names for things, before we said stone we sat on was chair but stone we slept on was bed and stone we wrote on stone with was pen and letter, though no letters had been written yet, address unknown.

We sat around under the round cold thing that made it possible for us to look deeply into one another's two small darker things, even though the round crackling thing that kept us warm had gone somewhere else again. We didn't have a name for the thing we were feeling, although we had taken our feeling on long vacations of tweaks and thuds.

So for no apparent prehistoric reason that I knew the name of, she touched (what I now know to be called) my buns, which made me feel warm, as if I had been touched by (what she now knows to be called) the sun, and blurted, "Zest! Ephemera! Buns!" To which I responded, "Why, yes! I have seen them!"

Our talk was small and absurd: a holy communion of saints, a forgiveness of sins, a resurrection of the body and of love everlasting. Although saying so never occurred to us, all warm and blurred, as we walked home across the tender stones, without a word.

ABOUT THE AUTHOR

Born in 1949, John Engman died in Minneapolis on December 10, 1996, from complications related to a congenital cerebral aneurysm. He earned a B.A. degree in English from Augsburg College in 1971 and a M.F.A. degree from the University of Iowa Writers' Workshop in 1975. His poems have appeared in a variety of publications, including these anthologies: *Leaving the Bough: 50 Younger American Poets* (International, 1982), *A Century in Two Decades* (Burning Deck Press, 1983), *Minnesota Writes: Poetry* (Milkweed Editions/Nodin Press, 1987), *The Best of Crazyhorse* (University of Arkansas Press, 1990), *New American Poets of the '90s* (David R. Godine, 1991), *The Decade Dance: A Celebration of Poems* (Sandhills Press, 1991), and *Atomic Ghost: Poets Respond to the Nuclear Age* (Coffee House Press, 1993). In 1980, *Alcatraz,* a chapbook, was published by Burning Deck Press; and in 1983, *Keeping Still, Mountain* was published by Galileo Press. Awards include a Minnesota State Arts Board Writing grant (1977); a Loft-McKnight Writers Award (1983-1984); a Bush Artist Fellowship (1987-1988); the Strousse Award, *Prairie Schooner* (1990); the Helen Bullis Award (co-winner), *Poetry Northwest* (1991); and a Loft-McKnight Award of Distinction (1996). He taught periodically in the writing programs at the University of Minnesota, St. Olaf College, and The Loft.